AVAILABLE NOW
from Lerner Publishing Services!

The *On the Hardwood* series:

Boston Celtics
Brooklyn Nets
Chicago Bulls
Dallas Mavericks
Houston Rockets
Indiana Pacers
Los Angeles Clippers
Los Angeles Lakers

Miami Heat
Minnesota Timberwolves
New York Knicks
Oklahoma City Thunder
Philadelphia 76ers
Portland Trail Blazers
San Antonio Spurs
Utah Jazz

COMING SOON!

Additional titles in
the *On the Hardwood* series:

Atlanta Hawks
Cleveland Cavaliers
Denver Nuggets
Detroit Pistons
Golden State Warriors
Memphis Grizzlies
Phoenix Suns
Washington Wizards

Lerner™

To Order • www.lernerbooks.com • 800-328-4929 • fax 800-332-1132

ON THE HARDWOOD

NEW YORK KNICKS

PETE BIRLE

On the Hardwood: New York Knicks

MVP Books
2255 Calle Clara
La Jolla, CA 92037

MVP Books is an imprint of Book Buddy Digital Media, Inc., 42982 Osgood Road, Fremont, CA 94539

MVP Books publications may be purchased for
educational, business, or sales promotional use.

Cover and layout design by Jana Ramsay
Copyedited by Susan Sylvia
Photos by Getty Images

ISBN: 978-1-61570-850-5 (Library Binding)
ISBN: 978-1-61570-834-5 (Soft Cover)

TABLE OF CONTENTS

Chapter 1
BASKETBALL CAPITAL OF THE WORLD

6

In the "City that Never Sleeps," everything moves faster. The lights shine brighter. The buildings are taller. And success, if you can achieve it, is always just a bit better.

That's why the New York Knickerbockers are always one of the most talked-about franchises in the National Basketball Association.

Forget the fact that the Knicks have only won two championships in their 65-plus years in the league. They are New York's team, the Big Apple's representative in the NBA. They play in Madison Square Garden, "The World's Most Famous Arena," just down the street

from the glitter of Times Square and Broadway. Celebrities from the theater, not to mention the movies and other pro sports, are always dropping by to be seen— and catch a game. New York native and film director Spike Lee is

The Knicks' most visible season ticket-holder, Spike Lee, is a fixture courtside at Madison Square Garden.

Thanks to its knowledgeable fans, the Knicks are constantly discussed, analyzed and criticized.

boroughs to the skyscrapers that dot the skyline of Lower Manhattan, New Yorkers love their basketball—and their home team. As a result, the Knicks receive a degree of attention that other teams don't—and don't want. They are constantly discussed, analyzed and criticized... by their own fans—on sports talk radio—as well as the media. Even when they have a poor season, they're talked about more than other teams with better records. It's both a blessing and a curse.

Back in 1970, sportswriter Pete Axthelm wrote a book called *The City Game,* shortly after the Knicks won their first NBA title. Two-thirds of the book is about

perhaps the team's most famous season ticket holder. You can see him regularly taunt opposing players while dressed in a Knicks jersey.

During the season, the Knicks are the talk of the town. From apartments in the outer

The City Game
Pete Axthelm's book describes how the playground legends of New York changed the way the game is played.

the team's championship season; the rest is about the playground legends that not only electrified the asphalt courts of New York but changed the way the game is played.

In his book, Axthelm writes about how basketball adapted well to the urban neighborhoods of Manhattan, Brooklyn, Queens, Staten Island, and the Bronx. The sport does not require as large a playing surface as, say, baseball or football. It can be played wherever a hoop can be hung, often with just two people. And it is ideal for youngsters of all economic backgrounds, because all you really need is a ball.

There is a love for basketball in New York that is tough to find

According to Axthelm, young athletes across the U.S. learn basketball, but city kids "live it."

Hoop Heaven

From some of the best high school teams in the nation to the legends ballin' on playgrounds, New York is the hotbed of hoops.

anywhere else. Sure, there are plenty of youngsters from the South, Midwest, and West who are ballers. But city kids grow up with a basketball in their hands—and a unique understanding and passion for the game. As Axthelm writes, "Other young athletes may learn basketball, but city kids live it."

For that reason, the Knicks are held to a higher standard by a fan base that knows basketball—and lives and dies with their team's every move. They play in a city with some of the best high school teams in the nation—and some of the greatest players no one has ever heard of. The special pride that the Knicks have brought New York is a feeling the playground warriors have always known.

Where else but New York can you watch Carmelo Anthony, Raymond Felton, and Tyson Chandler do their thing—then travel a few blocks to see a pick-up game featuring amateurs, often with even better moves.

The first pick in the 2012 NBA draft, Anthony Davis, chose a playground in New York for a photo shoot.

While New Yorkers will line the fences to watch a playground legend light it up, it's different inside the Garden. Nineteen thousand screaming fans rooting their team on can get loud. And when the Knicks are winning, there's no place in the world that can compare.

Hall of Fame Knickerbocker guard Walt Frazier knows it all too well.

"You make a few steals, or work a few good plays, and you have the feeling that it's going to be one of those nights," said Frazier. "The whole team gets into it, and then the crowd picks it up, and you come to the sidelines for a time-out and listen to that standing ovation, and it just makes you jingle inside."

The Knicks appreciate what it takes to win in New York, where the spotlight is always on. Like Frank Sinatra says in his signature song, if you can make it there, you'll make it anywhere.

Tyson Chandler receives approval from the Garden faithful.

11

NEWS photos by Dan Farrell

Wilt and Willis (foreground) head-to-head.

NEWS photo by John Duprey

Frazier goes up in first-half to score two of his game-high 36 points.

NEWS p

Walt Frazier
off his palm
second period
Powers i n d i
committed o
Jerry West (
tion to high
record-tying
Frazier, the
Bagdhad-on-t
played super

Kin
Of S

← Injure
all, Willis
guards Wilt
lain as The
pares to pa
teammate in
Reed, a quest
game, hit fir
though hobb
Knicks to f
pionship in th
113-99.

NEWS ph

As charter members of the NBA, the Knicks have more than six decades of history, tradition, heartbreak, and success.

Six of the 50 Greatest Players in NBA History were Knicks. Four of the 10 Greatest Coaches in league history guided the Knicks. And the 1970 championship team, which brought New York its first title, is considered one of the 10 Greatest Teams of all time.

It all began in 1946, when Madison Square Garden was granted a franchise in the newly-formed Basketball Association of America. (The BAA became the NBA in 1949.) Former sportswriter Ned Irish was the Knicks' founding father. He saw his franchise make the playoffs in each of their first nine seasons, losing in the NBA Finals three times. In year two, Joe Lapchick, the mastermind from St. John's, took over the coaching duties. The first agile big man in the NBA, Lapchick was enshrined in the NBA Hall of Fame in 1966 as a player. He also had 326 career victories as coach of the Knicks.

Joe Lapchick was already a legend at St. John's when he left to coach the Knicks.

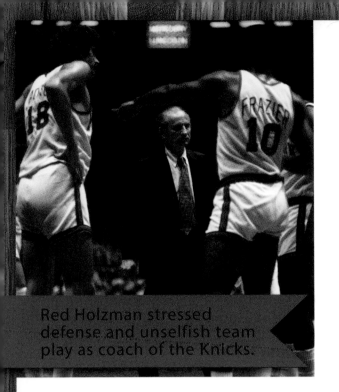

Red Holzman stressed defense and unselfish team play as coach of the Knicks.

The Knicks began to capture fans' attention in the early 1950s. Richie Guerin became one of the franchise's all-time favorite players by occasionally scoring 50 points a night. But New York had no big man to challenge the Celtics' Bill Russell or the 76ers' Wilt Chamberlain (who scored his 100 points against the Knicks in 1962).

That changed with the drafting of 6'9" center Willis Reed in 1964. Reed's impact was immediate. He was named Rookie of the Year in 1965. In 1966, the Knicks made it to the playoffs for the first time since 1959. The following year, New York added Frazier, Bill Bradley, and Head Coach William "Red" Holzman.

Holzman stressed a pressing and trapping defense, and he needed

But it took several years for the Knicks to steal the limelight from the college game. City schools New York University (NYU), St. John's, Fordham, Manhattan, and City College ruled the sports pages. And, every year, visiting teams from across the country descended on the Garden, nicknamed the "Mecca of College Hoops," for the National Invitation Tournament (NIT) championship.

one more piece to complete the puzzle. GM Eddie Donovan acquired Dave DeBusschere from Detroit, one of the league's best defensive forwards. Holzman, who grew up playing on the playgrounds of Manhattan's Lower East Side, now had the championship-caliber team he envisioned.

"We made some great trades, but this one has to be considered the best," said Holzman. "That made us a great team."

With a smothering defense that clogged the passing lanes and an offense that stressed hitting the open man, the Knicks were a balanced unit of role players. The result was four 50-plus-win seasons, three Eastern Conference championships, and two NBA titles.

It came together first in 1969-70. The Knicks finished the regular season 60-22. Reed became the first player ever to win the MVP for the regular season, All-Star game, and playoffs in the same year.

The Eastern Division champs knocked off the Baltimore Bullets in seven games in the first round of the post-season. They then beat the Milwaukee Bucks, with Kareem Abdul-Jabbar, in five. The Knicks' NBA Finals victory over the Lakers (with Hall of Famers Chamberlain, Jerry West, and Elgin Baylor) will forever be remembered for Reed hobbling out onto the court at

Seeing Red

Holzman is the only Knicks' coach to bring a championship to New York. A banner showing his 613 wins hangs at Madison Square Garden.

Willis Reed was a small center who more than made up for it with his physical style of play, clutch playoff performances, and soft touch from the outside.

Madison Square Garden for Game 7 despite a severely injured leg. As the Garden held its breath, Reed scored the game's initial bucket, and the crowd roared. Frazier tallied 36 points and 19 assists, and the Knicks captured their first NBA title with a 113-99 victory over Los Angeles.

"The Captain"

Reed, future Hall of Famer and one of the top 50 Greatest Players in NBA History, was the heart and soul of the Knicks' championship teams.

New York rallied around its newest professional heroes. In covering the Knicks, the New York media gave the sport its first real exposure. Like the playground legends admired across the city, the Knicks became larger than life.

Several became legendary NBA figures. First, there was Reed, nicknamed "The Captain." He was also the intimidator, willing to sacrifice personal glory for the good of the team. Once in the pros, Holzman's emphasis on defense and teamwork blended perfectly with Reed's game, which he had honed at Grambling State. The heart and soul of the Knicks, Reed set the tone for his teammates.

Frazier was a master defender and ball-handler. In his hometown of Atlanta, Frazier learned to dribble on a dirt court in all weather conditions. Following an impressive high school career, he accepted a basketball scholarship to Southern Illinois. But after losing his scholarship as a junior, Frazier had to pay his own way to school. He could only practice with the team. It was then he fell in love with defense.

"I had to practice it day in and day out," said Frazier. "Me and four other scrub guys, never playing any offense at all for a whole year."

Frazier made up the school credits and regained his eligibility for the 1966-67 season. He led the Salukis to the NIT title over Marquette.

When he got to New York, Frazier continued his exploits on

Walt Frazier was everything you'd want in a point guard: a master ball-handler, floor general, and defender.

Clyde

Frazier was the definition of cool: he wore designer suits, drove a Rolls Royce, and even had his own shoe: the Clyde.

the hardwood. But he became just as famous for his style off the court. He was nicknamed "Clyde" because he dressed like the gangster Clyde Barrow of the 1930s. Frazier would arrive at games in the fanciest of cars, a Rolls Royce. He would wear designer suits, broad-brimmed Italian hats, and full-length mink coats. He became the first NBA player to have his own signature shoe: the Clyde, made by Puma. (It's now in its fourth decade of production.) Frazier was the definition of cool.

Bradley—the future U.S. Senator from New Jersey—couldn't have been more different. He went to Princeton's prestigious Woodrow Wilson School of Public and International Affairs to study American history.

Although named College Player of the Year and the nation's most outstanding athlete, he walked away from basketball upon graduation to become a Rhodes Scholar at Oxford in England. Two years later, he signed with the Knicks for $500,000—a contract that earned him the nickname "Dollar Bill."

Bradley thrived with New York's brand of unselfish team basketball. Constantly moving around until he shook himself free, he was often the open man his teammates were looking for.

After the Knicks lured playground legend Earl "The Pearl"

Monroe away from division rival Baltimore in 1971, things got even better. Monroe and Frazier combined to form one of the greatest backcourts in NBA history. Though not as stylish a dresser as Clyde, the Pearl was flashier on the court.

The Knicks won their second NBA championship in 1973. They beat Baltimore and Boston in the playoffs to meet up with L.A. once again.

After losing Game 1, New York won the next four, holding the Lakers to fewer than 100 points in each contest. The Knicks became the first team in NBA history to defeat two 60-win teams en route to the title.

The Knicks were indeed something special.

From the playgrounds to center stage, Earl "The Pearl" Monroe always put on a show.

Chapter 3

The Beasts from the East

It would be a while before the Knicks made it back to the Finals (21 years, in fact), although they were always in the conversation.

Under Coach Hubie Brown, hometown hero Bernard King became the first Knick to lead the NBA in scoring with 32.9 points per game in 1984-85. But the playoff victories were few and far between —until something happened on Mother's Day, 1985.

On that day, the Knicks won the rights to seven-foot Georgetown University All-American center Patrick Ewing—in the first-ever NBA Lottery. Three months later, he signed the largest contract ever by an NBA rookie.

Ewing was born on the island of Jamaica, in the Caribbean. He was

raised in Trench Town, a poor area outside the capital city of Kingston. Growing up, he played cricket and soccer, where he used his wingspan and defensive tendencies to excel as a goalkeeper.

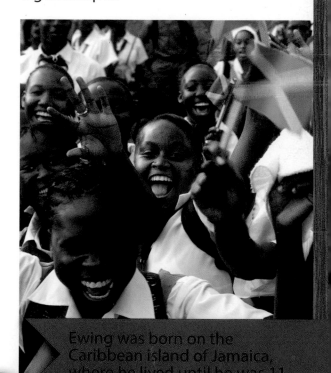

Ewing was born on the Caribbean island of Jamaica, where he lived until he was 11.

21

When he was eight years old, his mother moved to Cambridge, Massachusetts to find work. Ewing's dad joined her two years later. The rest of the Ewing family arrived, on their own or in pairs, over the next several years.

Patrick arrived in 1975 at the age of 11 and, from the start, had trouble adjusting. He had difficulty reading, and his Jamaican accent made it hard for his teachers to understand him. His mom enrolled him in the Achievement School for struggling junior high students. It was there Ewing played his first game of organized basketball.

By the time he started high school, he was 6'6" and showed tremendous promise. His high school coach, Mike Jarvis, introduced him to the team-first style of play made famous by the Boston Celtics.

"He became a star," Jarvis said of Ewing. "But he wasn't always a great player. He went through times where he was clumsy and

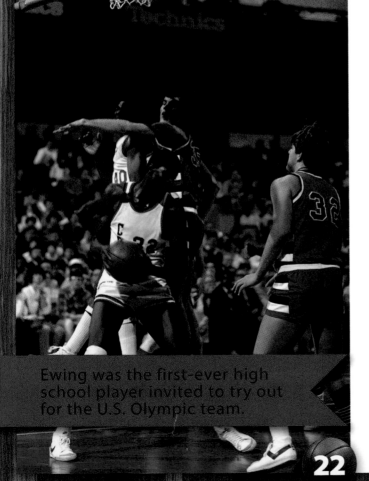

Ewing was the first-ever high school player invited to try out for the U.S. Olympic team.

awkward. We had to tell him to be tall, walk tall, be proud of it."

Ewing led his high school to three consecutive state championships. He was the first-ever high school player to be invited to try out for the Olympic team. (He didn't make it.) And he was the most sought-after senior in the nation. He chose to go to Georgetown, where

former Celtic John Thompson was coach. He led the Hoyas to three NCAA championship games and one national title. Nicknamed the "Hoya Destroya," Ewing was regarded as one of the greatest defensive players in college basketball history.

Ewing is regarded as one of the greatest college players of all time.

Once in New York, Ewing had his eyes on winning an NBA championship.

Despite Ewing's arrival and a 52-win season in 1989, the Knicks really didn't get on track until 1991, when new club president Dave Checketts hired Pat Riley. The coach had won nine Pacific Division titles and four NBA championships with the Los Angeles Lakers. Knicks fans agreed he belonged on the grandest stage of them all: New York.

Riley, in presiding over LA's reign, was the architect of "Showtime," the style of play that defined the Laker teams of the 1980s. Behind the no-look passes of their Magic Johnson-led fast-break offense, Riley's Lakers sold out arenas across the country while they established their dominance.

When he arrived in New York, Riley was already a pop-culture celebrity. Fond of wearing designer suits, slicking his hair back, and

The Winner Within

Things took off for the Knicks when coach Pat Riley arrived from L.A., where he had led the Lakers to four NBA titles.

sporting a year-round tan, Riley was perfect for the city and a Knicks team hungry for a title.

Only it wasn't "Showtime." Riley's Knicks employed a tenacious defense suited to the players on his roster and the legacy of the franchise. Their game plan was to score just enough points to win. The result: four consecutive 50-plus-win seasons, two Atlantic Division titles, a pair of trips to the Eastern Conference Finals, and several playoff series that captured the attention of the entire country. The Knicks' wars against the Bulls and the Pacers were epic battles.

The games featured plenty of "in your face" defense and enough clutch offensive performances to keep things at an intense level.

Riley was all style, but he had substance, too—just what Knicks fans were waiting for.

Spike Lee was on hand to help the Knicks give Michael Jordan of the Bulls and Reggie Miller of the Pacers all they could handle. Of course, the Garden fans loved it, chanting the team's now-famous rap/cheer over and over again: "Go New York, Go New York, Go."

In 1992-93, the Knicks won a team-record-tying 60 games and a club-record 37 home games. The following year, as one of the greatest defensive teams in NBA history (allowing just 91.5 points per game), the Knicks put together a dream season. Ewing, and fellow All-Stars Charles Oakley and John Starks, got help from a supporting cast that featured Anthony Mason, Charles Smith, Greg Anthony, Derek Harper, and Doc Rivers. And, as a result, New York finally defeated arch-rival Chicago to reach the NBA Finals.

Anthony Mason, a tough forward, played tenacious defense and took the game to the opponent.

But, in a grueling seven-game series where neither team scored more than 100 points, the Knicks lost to Hakeem Olajuwon and the Houston Rockets.

They came back the next year, but lost another classic seven-game Eastern Conference Final series to Indiana. The final game proved to be one of Ewing's—and the Knicks'—most heartbreaking. With just seconds to go, and the Pacers up by two, Ewing missed a finger roll that would have tied the game. The loss was especially devastating to Riley, who stepped down as coach the day after the NBA Finals ended.

Starks' dunk over Jordan in the 1993 Eastern Conference Finals increased the rivalry between the two teams.

Chapter 4

A Team of Destiny

After leaving New York, Riley headed south to coach the Miami Heat (and serve as their general manager, too). As a result, an intense rivalry between the Knicks and the Heat was born.

Theirs quickly became one of the NBA's fiercest rivalries. It was a match-up of two physical, defensive-minded teams, with Ewing squaring off against fellow Georgetown center Alonzo Mourning. The Knicks and Heat met in the Eastern Conference Semifinals in 1996-97 in what turned out to be the first of several playoff slugfests between the two Atlantic Division foes.

The Knicks took Game 1 in Miami and Games 3 and 4 in New York. Game 5 was marred by an incident between the Heat's P.J. Brown and

The Heat is On
The Knicks and the Miami Heat developed one of the NBA's fiercest rivalries in the late 1990s.

the Knicks' Charlie Ward. Starks, Ewing, Larry Johnson, and Allan Houston left the bench. As a result, Brown was suspended for the rest of the series. Ewing, Houston, and

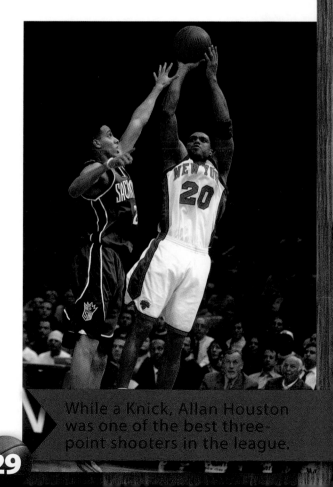

While a Knick, Allan Houston was one of the best three-point shooters in the league.

DEFENCE!

The 1998-99 Knicks played a defensive style of ball that typified the franchise: physical, hard-nosed, and workmanlike.

Ward were suspended for Game 6, and Johnson and Starks were suspended for Game 7.

The Heat won the series and, from that point forward, every game

Charles Oakley was an intimidating presence on defense.

between the two teams over the next few years was an outright war. They met in the playoffs the next three years in a row, with each series going the full number of games, be it five or seven.

Under the guidance of Coach Jeff Van Gundy, the Knicks continued to emphasize the defense that had come to define the franchise. While there may not be much defense on the playgrounds across the city, inside the Garden it was in full supply. From Ewing on down the roster, the Knicks played a physical, hard-nosed, workmanlike game of basketball.

First, there was Oakley, who was known as a defensive specialist. If the Knicks needed someone to shut down an opposing player, "Oak" usually got the assignment. Starks, who attended four different colleges in his native Oklahoma and was not drafted, was the Knicks' poster child for physical play. Undaunted, Starks would take on anyone. Together with Ewing and Oakley, Starks helped to keep the Knicks' defense in their opponents' face.

At 36 years old, Ewing made one last trip to the NBA Finals in the lockout-shortened 1998-99 season. It was an amazing chapter in Knickerbocker history. New York went from a team in turmoil to a team of destiny.

Coming off four straight seasons in which they lost in the Eastern

Along with Oakley and Ewing, Starks wasn't afraid to get physical.

Conference Semifinals, the Knicks made some moves. Before the season even began, they traded two of

Swan Song

Ewing made one final go at a championship in 1999. They were the first eighth seed to ever reach the NBA Finals.

31

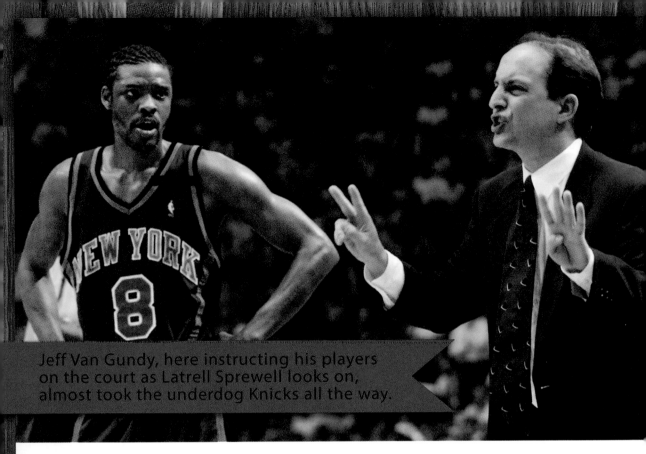

Jeff Van Gundy, here instructing his players on the court as Latrell Sprewell looks on, almost took the underdog Knicks all the way.

their most popular players, Oakley and Starks, in an attempt to get younger. Initially, fans complained. But the two players they acquired soon had all of New York cheering.

An Even Swap

Initially, Knicks fans didn't like the trade: Starks and Oakley for Latrell Sprewell and Marcus Camby. But soon they were cheering.

Marcus Camby and Latrell Sprewell turned out to be better than advertised. They teamed with Ewing, Larry Johnson, and Allan Houston, and as a result, the Knicks were suddenly a dangerous team.

They didn't show it right away, though. With a record of 21-21 at one point and in danger of missing the playoffs outright, the Knicks suddenly got hot. A victory over Miami, after being down by 20 in the second half, was the turning point of the season. New York ended up earning the eighth and final playoff spot in the East.

Not expected to advance, the Knicks beat that same Miami team in the first round of the playoffs. Ewing got the best of Mourning, as the two big men pitted their respective defensive prowess against each other. The Knicks won Game 5 on a last-second shot by Houston that bounced off the front of the rim and fell through.

They then swept the Atlanta Hawks, which meant an Eastern Conference Final matchup vs. Indiana. Even after Ewing went down in Game 2 with an injured Achilles' tendon, the Knicks took Game 3, thanks to Johnson's four-point play with 5.7 seconds left. They then won Games 5 and 6 to stun the Pacers and earn a trip to the NBA Finals.

Waiting there were the San Antonio Spurs and their "Twin Towers" David Robinson and Tim Duncan.

Down three games to one and at home, the Knicks gave their fans a memory to last a lifetime. Latrell Sprewell staged an offensive duel with Duncan that, to this day, is one of the most exciting in NBA Finals history.

A Storybook Post-Season

Not expected to advance, the eighth-seeded Knicks beat the Heat, the Hawks, and the Pacers in the playoffs to earn a trip to the 1999 NBA Finals.

Sprewell had come to New York in 1999 after serving a suspension for an altercation with his former coach at Golden State, P.J. Carlesimo. He had to win over the often-critical Garden crowd. He did, and then some, with his overall intensity throughout the season and his classic battle with Duncan in the Finals.

The Spurs had their hands full containing the 6'5" Sprewell, who scored 25 of the Knicks' last 34 points. When New York was down 47-43, "Spree" then scored and was fouled on a driving dunk for a three-point play. Two consecutive jumpers gave him seven consecutive points in a minute and a half to pull the Knicks even at 50.

In the fourth quarter, the two went at it like a pair of heavyweight boxers. First, Duncan would score. Then, Sprewell would answer. And back and forth they went… until the final two seconds of the game, with the Spurs

Sprewell put on a show in Game 5 of the 1999 NBA Finals, dueling with the Spurs' Tim Duncan.

clinging to a 78-77 lead.

That's when Spree, pinned under the basket, launched a desperation shot over the outstretched arms of Duncan. With the Garden at a fever pitch, the ball fell short of the rim as the buzzer sounded. The Knicks came up empty while the Spurs won their first NBA title.

Despite Sprewell's heroics, without Ewing (and with Johnson plagued by a bad back), the Knicks were simply no match for San Antonio's "Twin Towers."

The Ewing era was over. After more than 1,000 games in 15 years, it ended with the center becoming the all-time club leader in just about every category. While he wasn't able to deliver a championship to New York, Patrick Ewing goes down in history as arguably the greatest Knick ever.

DAILY SPORTS NEW

NEW YORK'S NO. 1 SPORTS SECTION

GREATEST

On Ewing's night, Willis calls Patrick best Knick ever

Ewing retired from the Knicks the club leader in just about every offensive and defensive category.

Chapter 5

RETURN TO GLORY

Trouble befell the Knicks once Ewing departed in 2000. High salaries made players difficult to trade, and salary cap problems limited the franchise's ability to sign free agents.

As a result, the last decade was a rough one—by anyone's standards, much less the demanding New York fan base. The Knicks only made three trips to the playoffs, losing in the first round each time. But the 2012-13 Knicks were primed to build off several blockbuster acquisitions and a healthy dose of "Linsanity."

First, there was the arrival in 2010 of All-Star power forward and 2003 NBA Rookie of the Year, Amar'e Stoudamire. On the first day that free agents were allowed to sign, the Knicks introduced Stoudamire at Madison Square Garden. Reunited with head coach Mike D'Antoni, who had coached him in Phoenix, Stoudamire vocally shared

Things started to turn around for the Knicks when Carmelo Anthony and Amar'e Stoudamire arrived in New York.

Tyson Chandler was the NBA's Defensive Player of the Year in 2011-12.

New York started to buzz.

It reached a fever pitch when the front office traded for Carmelo Anthony in February of 2011. The 6'8" "Melo" is one of the NBA's most explosive offensive talents, and one of the top pure shooters in the league. His pairing with Stoudamire gave New York fans something they didn't have a lot of recently: a reason to believe.

"… We kinda grew up in the same era… and we took the league by storm as young players," said Stoudamire. "Now for us to be here in New York, on a bigger stage, it's going to be great, it's going to be fun."

Then, when Tyson Chandler arrived in December 2011, Knicks fans could hardly contain their

his optimism about the Knicks' returning to the top of the Eastern Conference. He publicly proclaimed, "The Knicks are back!" The city of

enthusiasm. The 7'1" center, one of the year's top free agents, had just helped the Mavericks win their first NBA championship. He joined the Knicks as part of a three-way sign-and-trade with the Mavs and Wizards.

"I know what my job is coming here," Chandler said upon arriving in New York. "I know I came here to defend. I'm going to defend the rim, I'm going to rebound, I'm going to get extra shots. And I think if we play on both ends, and play as a team, the sky is definitely the limit for this squad."

Adding to the excitement was the play in 2012 of undrafted D-League prospect Jeremy Lin, who came out of nowhere to ignite the team—and the Big Apple. Having been let go

Fans were immediately caught up in the "Linsanity."

by Golden State and Houston, Lin wasn't sure he even had a future in the NBA. He was ready to either try his luck in Europe or take a break from the game altogether.

With some key injuries at the guard position, the Knicks took a chance on the Harvard grad— the first American-born player of Chinese descent. In a stretch of just 26 games, Lin charmed not just New York but the world by posting averages of 18.5 points, 7.7 assists, 3.7 steals and two rebounds. The Knicks immediately went 7-0 upon Lin's insertion in the lineup. He dropped 38 against the Lakers and beat Toronto with a buzzer-beater. In the process, he became a global sensation.

After the Linsanity

Once Lin left for Houston, the Knicks made some big moves. The result: a talented roster, and the oldest team in the history of the NBA.

"I haven't done a computation, but it's fair to say that no player has created the interest and the frenzy in this short period of time, in any sport, that I'm aware of, like Jeremy Lin has," said NBA Commissioner David Stern.

Lin signed a contract with Houston following the 2011-12 campaign, and now plays for the Rockets. But New York made some moves in the off-season to further bolster its roster. Key additions included future Hall of Famer Jason Kidd, Raymond Felton, and Marcus Camby, back for a second go-around with the Knicks. As such, New York is a talented team that has set its sights on making a deep run into the playoffs.

Led by Mike Woodson, who took

over in March 2012 when D'Antoni resigned, the Knicks are experienced, with a corps of battle-tested veterans. The average age of the Knicks is 32.66 years, which makes them the oldest team in the history of the NBA. Pablo Prigioni, Rasheed Wallace, Camby, Kidd, and Kurt Thomas are all over 35.

There's no doubt, however, that their leader is small forward Anthony. Melo is a native New Yorker, born in the Red Hook projects in Brooklyn to a Puerto Rican father and an African-American mother. His dad, after whom he is named, died of cancer when Anthony was two years old. When he turned eight, his family moved to Baltimore.

Jason Kidd was a mentor for guards Raymond Felton, J.R. Smith, and Iman Shumpert.

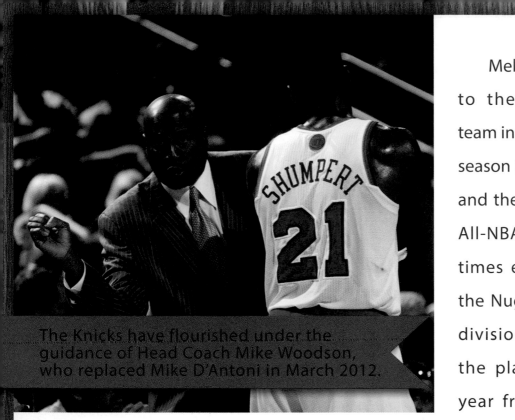

The Knicks have flourished under the guidance of Head Coach Mike Woodson, who replaced Mike D'Antoni in March 2012.

After a successful high school career, Melo attended Syracuse, where he led the Orangemen to their first National Championship in 2003 as a freshman. After earning the tournament's Most Outstanding Player award, Anthony left college to enter the NBA Draft, where he was selected with the third pick by the Denver Nuggets.

Melo was named to the All-Rookie team in his inaugural season in the league, and the All-Star and All-NBA teams five times each. He led the Nuggets to two division titles and the playoffs every year from 2004 to 2010. In 2009, he helped the Nuggets advance to the Conference Finals for the first time since 1985.

Anthony also won a bronze medal at the 2004 Olympics and gold medals at the 2008 and 2012 Olympics. On Aug. 2, 2012, he broke the U.S. Men's Olympic Team record for most points in a single game with

37 points against Nigeria.

What Melo does best is put the ball in the basket. Equally strong and quick, he is difficult to stop in the open court or one-on-one. According to Stephen A. Smith of ESPN, Anthony is one of the NBA's elite.

"Melo has a mid-range game, a long-range game, he can score off the dribble, or he can spot up, and he can post up, too," said Smith. "He's a defender's worst nightmare."

Anthony has struggled at times sharing the ball and making good decisions down the stretch. But there's no questioning his ability. He could be the one

who takes the Knicks back to "the Promised Land," said Smith.

Now, back in his hometown

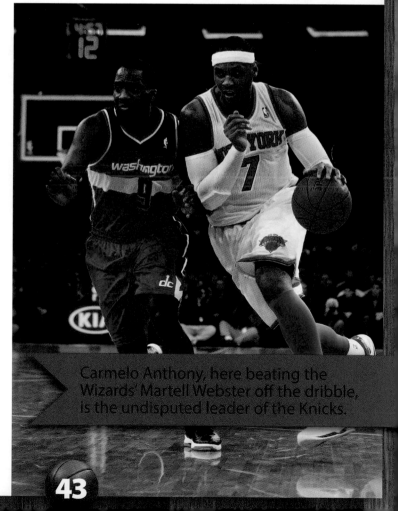

Carmelo Anthony, here beating the Wizards' Martell Webster off the dribble, is the undisputed leader of the Knicks.

Anthony, born in Brooklyn, likes the rivalry that is forming between the two New York teams.

vaulted to first place in the Eastern Conference. By April, he had locked up the 2012-13 NBA scoring title. One thing was clearly evident to the New York fans: Melo was having fun.

"I smile all the time, even when I'm in a bad mood," said Melo. "I always try to keep a smile on my face."

Knicks fans were smiling, too—especially because the team was back to its winning ways. It wasn't just because of Melo, though. Point guard Felton is a pick-and-roll ace, who works his magic with Chandler on a nightly basis. And when Chandler, the

playing for the Knicks, Melo has vowed to improve on defense and to trust his teammates in crunch time. He started the year true to his word and immediately entered the argument for MVP—as the Knicks

league's Defensive Player of the Year in 2011-12, is on his game, the Knicks are a top-five defensive team. Add shooting guard Iman Shumpert to that mix and New York may even rank higher.

On the offensive end, 6'10" Steve Novak can break games wide open with his skillful shooting from three-point range. And guard J.R. Smith turned out to be the best sixth man in the league, embracing Woodson's team style of play and maturing both on and off the court.

"This year it's been more serious," said Smith. "I understand every road trip we take is a work trip, not just a play trip. You come and work hard."

Iman Shumpert, here guarding Paul Pierce of the Boston Celtics, was the only rookie to receive votes for Defensive Player of the Year in 2011-12.

Amar'e Stoudemire, who has had his fair share of setbacks, is a survivor. And New York likes survivors.

due to back pain. Hurt once again, New York fans are hoping the impact player returns to his previous form… and soon.

This Knickerbocker team could very well bring another title home to New York. And now that a rivalry with the Brooklyn Nets is brewing in the Big Apple, a Knicks team that contends for the crown will have everyone talking.

Not that they wouldn't be chatting anyway, because basketball is the city game. And the Knicks are always in the conversation.

Stoudamire is no stranger to working hard. Coming off knee surgery, he spent the summer of 2012 trying to forget the previous winter—when he lost his brother in a car crash, and lost his flexibility

Today's Knicks are a scrappy unit that prides itself on playing team defense – and aims on returning to the NBA Finals to win another title for New York.